I0785810

UNDERSTANDING
Globalism

What is
the "New World Order"?

Frank N. Mitchell

This UNDERSTANDING booklet is part of a series of booklets on key issues of our time on the Reign of Christ at
www.ashiningcityonahill.org
www.reignofchrist.org
All booklets are available at amazon.com

September 2018

UNDERSTANDING
Globalism
What is the "New World Order"?

Today, we often hear the term "globalism" used by political commentators, and it is often associated with the idea of some sort of ominous "New World Order." However, in my experience these terms are often not really used with any precision or precise definition. And, worst still, people who decry any sort of globalism or New World Order often seem to have a very narrow nationalist view of world affairs.

For example, I personally have heard many people over the years say America should get out of the United Nations. This has always struck me as a very bizarre thing to say. I mean who can be against world peace or against an international body like the United Nations that tries to preserve world peace as its very reason for being? Over many past years, I have thought nobody in their right mind would think these sorts of things about world affairs. With these thoughts in my head, some months ago now, I did a systematic study of the interrelated topics of globalism, the New World Order, and the United Nations, and I was in fact shocked at what I discovered as I began to connect all the various dots of history over the last three hundred years or so.

3

Globalism and the New World Order
"Globalism" generally refers to the free movement of goods, services, capital, and people around the globe between nations, which on the surface sounds like not such a terrible thing. In fact, on the surface, it sounds like a pretty good thing, but this is only on the surface. The specifics of "free movement" can quickly become a somewhat complicated matter because implicitly globalism by definition (free movement of virtually everything) tends to undermine sovereign nation-states.

By contrast, the term "New World Order" does **not** usually have a set meaning, just the opposite, because it tends to refer to any point in history of dramatic shifts in international relations between nations in international politics such as post World War I when the phrase was first used in our time by Woodrow Wilson, and the phrase was used at the end of the Cold War by G. H. W. Bush. However, in actual history, the term "New World Order" can, in fact, have very specific definitions that vary widely, for good and for ill.

America's founding
To get the whole picture on globalism and a New World Order one must go back to the founding of America, which was seen by the American founders to be an example model nation of what a nation-state could be with the consent of the governed and equal rights for all and with Liberty and Justice for all based on the Higher Moral Law or what Jefferson

called the moral "Laws of Nature and of Nature's God." The 1776 American founders saw this to be God's will for government as outlined by the social political philosopher John Locke, and many of the founders were what is called Fifth Monarchists, meaning they saw themselves as doing the actual Reign of Christ of Bible prophecy for the nation-state based on the book of Daniel in the Bible.

And, famously, Jefferson said America was the world's best hope for this achievement of having a nation based on the moral Laws of Nature and of Nature's God, and Lincoln famously added America was the world's last best hope for such a nation. And the Great Seal of the United States has the Latin phrase NOVUS ORDO SECLORIUM, which translated means New Order of the Ages, which the American founders saw 1776 to be creating in a very good and positive sense.

Though there were some notable exceptions, up until the 1688 Glorious Revolution in Britain, absolute monarchy had generally been the order of the day in the West since the fall of the Roman Empire. The Glorious Revolution was also based on the teachings and philosophy of John Locke, but in the course of history Britain and America tended to be **exceptional** in being constitutional democracies based on the moral Laws of Nature and of Nature's God and not having absolute monarchies, and in effect creating a New Order of the Ages.

Woodrow Wilson and World War I
What happens in history is the devastation of World War I seems to bring the era of absolute monarchies to an end on a worldwide basis. As Woodrow Wilson said, America was fighting World War I to "make the world safe" for American-style democracies, thus fulfilling the hopes and dreams of the American founders to have America be the model for all nations of the world in a new order of the ages, so to speak.

The significance of this for Bible prophecy and the Kingdom of God come on Earth cannot be overstated. With the end of World War I and a possible League of Nations, it seemed that the Fifth Monarchists' dream could take place not just in America but worldwide with free sovereign states harmoniously, prosperously, and peaceably interacting on a worldwide basis. And the idea was the League of Nations would secure that world peace and world order.

Woodrow Wilson called this a "New World Order" to replace balance of power politics of nation-states of mostly highly undesirable absolute monarchies. In reality Woodrow Wilson's use of the term New World Order was pretty clearly meant to refer to an *actual* Judeo-Christian millennialism come on Earth to create a New Order of the Ages that the American founders had dreamed of. The League of Nations, however, was not really going to be able to guarantee world peace as Wilson envisioned it, and

Germany and Japan were not, all things considered, ready for an American-style democracy at that time.

Further, America did not even join the League of Nations because of the famous Article X of the League, which gave the League of Nations the right to declare war or obligate nations to war against rogue nations. Wilson would not compromise on this provision I think because without it the League would seem to have no teeth, but in reality no nation can reasonably give up its right to declare war to some international body, and so the Treaty of Versailles was rightly rejected by America.

Marx's counter-vision of a New World Order
It is in this period between the two World Wars with the failure of the League of Nations to keep world peace that the idea of a "New World Order" gets very bizarre, and it comes to mean anything but free sovereign states in harmonious interaction throughout the world as Wilson had envisioned. To understand the strange twist that happened to the term New World Order between the two World Wars, one must go back to the previous century.

In the 19th century Karl Marx had famously rejected the American founding and its vision for good government. The American founding was based on theism (rights from God), and it had three major components: Justice, Righteousness and the free sovereign state based on the moral Laws of Nature and of Nature's God, which was to be a model for the nations for an actual Judeo-Christian millennialism that was to be the New Order of the Ages. This is very simple and very straightforward.

However, Marx was famously an atheist. And as even the atheist philosopher Bertrand Russell pointed out Marx with his world communism in effect comes up with a counter-millennialism (or anti-millennialism) to Judeo-Christian millennialism. Marx's anti-millennialism was based on atheism (with no rights from God) and in place of the Justice of private property and free enterprise and getting to keep the fruits of one's labor, Marx comes up with an anti-Justice of collectivism with no rights to private property or free enterprise or getting to keep the fruits of one's labor. The state is to confiscate all wealth and the fruits of all labor in order to redistribute all wealth to the collective.

For Righteousness Marx has an anti-Righteousness of hedonism, no family values, and the children belong to the state with the traditional family just being a tool of exploitative capitalism. And for free sovereign states there will be **a one-world government for a worldwide "dictatorship of the proletariat."** This is pretty standard stuff for understanding Marx, but what is interesting here and not always commented on is Marx thought that all traditional concepts of Justice and Righteousness (superstructure he calls them) were just empty verbiage to justify power structures of the ruling class.

To be blunt here, Marx thought, in effect, "might was right" and whoever is in charge (whether aristocracy or capitalists or proletariat) sets up a "dictatorship" to lord power over the other classes. Everything for Marx was a matter of class conflict and one class winning out over another in violent revolution. Marx had *no* concern with justice or injustice. This is pretty basic Marxism here, and as Ronald Reagan said famously and correctly Marx's communism is not an economic system but a form insanity. Why? Because in this economic system everyone will be a proletariat worker working in slave labor for subsistence wages with *no* rights and with *no* freedom of speech, press or religion. This communism of Marx was *openly* to be a true hell-on-earth in what is known as a dehumanizing dystopia. This was to be the Communism of 1917 Russia.

A New Marxist Collectivism
However, in the late 19th century, there were other atheists who were *also* collectivists, and they agreed with Marx that capitalism, private property, free enterprise, the family, the nation-state, and even individuality were all basically self-evident evils. This means, in effect, that all the larger concepts of traditional Justice and Righteousness based on the moral **Laws of Nature and of Nature's God were *also* self-evident evils as were the nations founded on those laws, as Britain and America had been in 1688 and 1776 respectively.** (For more on this see

the booklet "UNDERSTANDING Alternative Political Universes.")

However, in opposition to Marx, these other atheist communist collectivists did **not** believe in violence and class conflict as Marx had. In fact, they were utopian pacifists, and they believed in total disarmament, and they believed in establishing world communism not by violence but at the ballot box. And they did not believe that might makes right but rather right makes might, but they as atheists did **not** believe in traditional concepts of Justice and Righteousness based on the moral Laws of Nature and of Nature's God, so they came up with a substitute moral standard, namely, "the universal brotherhood of man" to keep from having a dystopian hell-on-earth as Marx had based on slave labor, violence, and dictatorship of the strongest class.

For these pacifist utopian communist collectivists everything that supports the universal brotherhood of man is morally good (in their new "morality"), and anything that does not support the universal brotherhood of man is morally evil. In this non-violent utopian (not dehumanizing dystopian) communism, the universal brotherhood of man is the standard by which all things will be judged. For example, capitalism exploits people (the brotherhood) because one person has to work for another. So, capitalism is an evil. These utopian collectivists held everyone should work for the collective in selfless service and not for his own individual gain by supposedly exploiting others.

Further, this utopian communism will have freedom of speech, press, and religion, but it will be limited to politically correct speech, press, and religion that promotes the universal brotherhood of man, and any speech, press or religion that does not promote the universal brotherhood of man will be divisive of the brotherhood and will be, in essence, hate-speech, hate-press, or hate-religion, and it will not allowed. This prohibited speech will potentially include all traditional concepts of Justice and Righteousness, God, Christianity, and the Gospel as supposedly bigoted, prejudiced, and so forth. This means that this utopian communism has freedom of speech, press, and religion in name only for all practical purposes.

In this non-violent pacifist communism established at the ballot box, not by violent revolution, **every person in the world is due an equal share of the world's wealth and resources based on their equal humanity as part of the universal brotherhood of man**, and this also makes for citizens of the world and not citizens of nation-states. In the hard communism of Marx one's identity was in being a member of the worldwide proletariat and its one-world government. In this utopian communism one's identity is in being a citizen of the world (not citizen of a nation-state) with a one-world communist government based on the worldwide brotherhood of man.

And in this new utopian communism (except for a few years of youth service), no one is in slave labor as in Marx. In fact, no one has to work at all. Why? Because everyone has a basic human right to an equal share of the world's wealth and resources by virtue of their humanity, and working has nothing to do with it. All work will be voluntary in service to the collective, and one gets no pay check because one is already getting one's equal share of the world's wealth, and if one does get a paycheck, it will be divided out equally among the world's population.

When everyone gets what they have coming to them for free by virtue of their common humanity in this utopian socialist or collectivist brotherhood, **that is called Social Justice** (meaning Socialist "Justice"), or it is sometimes called Economic Justice or Distributive Justice, **and** one has a basic (positive) "human right" to that equal share in this utopian worldwide communism where no one has to work. And, as we have just seen, there will be no **real** freedom of speech, press and religion, but only phony politically correct freedom of speech, press and religion, and as with Marx's communism there will be no free enterprise, no private property, no individuality, and no individual rights or freedoms of the Glorious Revolution and American Revolution based on the moral Laws of Nature. As in the old

Marxist communism, we are to all be nameless faceless numbers with no individuality, but in this new communism we are to live in worldwide utopian indulgence not working a day in our lives outside of a few years youth service.

Socialist Democracy, the Third Way
This utopian non-violent communism goes by a series of different labels. It is called social democracy, meaning socialism by democratic voting not by violence. It is also called "the third way" since it rejects both capitalism as well as a hard communism by violence. Sometimes it is called Fabian Socialism, and sometimes the new Radicalism or the New Liberalism.

Rather than plotting a violent revolution as Lenin did, these social democrats plan to teach their communist utopian agenda in all the schools and churches as a good in order to create voters to implement it as a political agenda in voting for Social Justice candidates in order to distribute all the world's wealth by a world government to make all people of the world economically equal whether they work or not because of the universal brotherhood of man or family of man. To accomplish this for the social democrats there is to be a basic drill or catechism for all the churches and all the schools:

Capitalism and free enterprise are an evil; utopian socialism and its Social Justice are a good. All individuality is an evil and inherently selfish, but new socialist man living only for the collective and the brotherhood of man is a good. Traditional freedom of speech, press and religion are evils and are hateful and bigoted, but all-inclusive non-judgmental pc speech, press, and religion are goods. The nation-state is an evil and causes wars, but one-world socialist government is a good, and it stops wars and distributes all wealth and resources equally worldwide. All guns and armaments are an evil and cause wars, and ending all guns and armaments worldwide is a good and will stop all war because there can be no war if there are no guns and armaments.

The idea of these nutty utopian socialists was if you teach all of this nonsense in the schools and churches within a generation or two you can have an actual communist revolution by the vote, not firing a shot, and it will thereby overthrow the governments of the Glorious Revolution in Britain and the American Revolution in America based on the moral Laws of Nature and of Nature's God with traditional Liberty and Justice for all. And when all the nations have such revolutions by the ballot box, they will then all agree to form a one-world governmental authority over all the nations of the world in order to effectively end all traditional rights and freedoms and to end the nation-state for a worldwide utopian socialism to do the worldwide Social Justice with the equal worldwide wealth redistribution as it has been taught in the schools and churches for years.

This utopian communism is a false millennialism that in the end is as bad as the false millennialism of Marx because in the end it has not only no free enterprise or private property but also no **real** freedom of speech, press and religion, and these utopian socialists concede that if not enough people want to volunteer to work for no pay to produce the necessary goods and resources for the world to function, then there will have to be worldwide "universal conscription" of the world's population in forced slave labor in order to produce all the world's goods and services so we do not all starve to death or freeze to death, etc. So, in the end, it is the same damn communism as Marx had except it is to be established not by violent revolution of the proletariat but at the ballot box by people voting for Social Democrat candidates to do Social Justice, which is one's positive human right to an equal share of the world's wealth based on the false moral standard of the universal brotherhood of man.

These socialist democrats between the two World Wars start to call their worldwide socialist government (with **no** traditional individual rights and freedoms) a "New World Order" to **replace** Wilson's "New World Order" of free sovereign states harmoniously interacting in peace and prosperity in a true, not false, Judeo-Christian millennialism. These socialists argue as World War II begins that the Treaty of Versailles had failed to keep the peace and avoid another World War **because** it had left three things intact, namely, capitalism, the nation-state, and armaments, all three of which these socialists had been arguing against for a good fifty plus years by the 1930s.

These social democrats felt the economic crash of 1929, the Great Depression, and the rise of Hitler proved them correct in their agenda for a one-world government to end capitalism, the nation-state, and all armaments worldwide and to implement worldwide Social Justice with equal wealth redistribution as a *new* "New World Order" to replace the New World Order of free sovereign states that Wilson had proposed. These socialist democrats called for a *new* League of Nations to follow World War II, and it will ultimately be called **the United Nations**, which will be formed as a one-world governmental authority to implement this entire worldwide utopian Socialist Justice agenda of no nation-states, no borders, no armaments, no private property or free enterprise and with no traditional individual rights and freedoms but only false positive humanist rights.

H. G. Wells' "Third Way" New World Order
Incredibly, this plan is explicitly outlined by the socialist democrat H. G. Wells in 1940 in his book actually entitled *The New World Order* in which he openly appeals to FDR to champion this agenda for this new League of Nations to follow the war, and in 1941 FDR does just that for all practical purposes in his famous Four Freedoms speech, and he does it again in his famous economic positive rights speech

in 1944. If you read the United Nations Charter and the subsequent Universal Declaration of Human Rights, they are basically just a rehash of FDR's two speeches and of Wells' book *The New World Order.*

The United Nations was actually formed to be a worldwide socialist governmental authority to effectively end all nation-states, all borders, all armaments, and all capitalism, and all of these things are to be replaced by a world government authority, the UN, doing worldwide utopian Social Justice and its positive rights to an equal share of the world's wealth based on the universal brotherhood of man. It seems likely this outrageous UN construction as we know it would never have happened if Wells had not written his nutty utopian communist book and if FDR had not taken up the cause and used his position as president of the United States to push the United Nations through to completion. However, almost all of this is not generally known.

The Story of the United Nations
There are numerous reasons why almost none of this incredible story of the United Natons is generally known. What are some of those reasons? First, the UN charter got rid of the famous Article X of the League of Nations, and this is what had been America's main concern.

Second, the foundational principle of the universal brotherhood of man is mentioned just to start things, but the Universal Declaration quickly shifts to the rights to equal wealth redistribution in positive rights with little emphasis on the equal aspect of the redistribution. Also, the United Nations Charter and Universal Declaration talk of broad social, economic and education socialist "rights" but only in vague general terms to be achieved in the coming years, which all the nations of the world are committing to.

And finally the United Nations Charter and Universal Declaration do exactly what FDR did, namely, they first list traditional rights as one would find in the US Bill of Rights, but these all tend to be negated for all practical purposes by the later positive human rights of the universal brotherhood of man that are added and listed later in the UN founding documents. For example, one has a right to private property **unless** the state decides you do not. One has a right to freedom of expression **unless** it speaks against the positive human rights of others, etc.

In Summary
In summary, in fact, besides having a general meaning of a dramatic shift in international relations at some given time in history, "New World Order" has the three major and specific formulations in history each with its own distinct millennial vision as we have seen so far. There is a fourth formulation we will look at below, and it is called corporatist globalism (or corporatism) for a New World Order of transnational corporations. So, the four major and

very specific formulations of a New World Order are the following:

First Formulation:
The American Founding
The first formulation is the American founding vision of the Fifth Monarchists of the Reign of Christ come on Earth where there are free sovereign states with Justice and Righteousness based on the moral Laws of Nature and of Nature's God, Wisely applied by the statesman legislator for the common good or general welfare of the commonwealth, and the nations of the world live in harmonious interaction and in peace and prosperity in a clear fulfillment of Judeo-Christian millennialism.

Second Formulation:
The Hard Communism of Marx
The second formulation is the hard Communism of Marx. It is an alternative dystopian counter-millennialism to Judeo-Christian millennialism. Without using the term, this is the New World Order position of Marx based on materialism and atheism with a one-world government and no free sovereign states, and that government has a counter anti-Justice of collectivism with no private property or free enterprise and a counter anti-Righteousness with no traditional personal morality or family values. And there is no freedom of speech, press or religion, and we all live in slave labor for subsistence wages in what is called the tyranny or "dictatorship" of the proletariat. This second New World Order is usually

called Marxist Leninism, and as noted above, as Reagan said, it is not really a form of economics but a form of insanity.

Third Formulation:
"Third Way" Communism of Socialist Democrats
The "third way" utopian New World Order communist socialism of Wells, FDR, the UN, and social democrats generally is also a counter-millennialism to the Judeo-Christian millennialism of Locke and Jefferson and the revolutions of 1688 and 1776, and it is a non-violent (pacifist) Marxist collectivism also with a one-world government and no free sovereign states. This world government also has a counter false anti-Justice of collectivism, and it is called "Social Justice" with no private property or free enterprise, and there is also the same counter anti-Righteousness with no traditional personal morality or family values, but all of this is be established by the vote at the ballot box and not by violent revolution.

This collectivism is **not** based on the truly nutty idea of dialectical materialism (as Marx had done) but on a supposed new higher consciousness moral standard of the universal brotherhood of man to replace the traditional moral standard of the Golden Rule (or Second Great Commandment). In this collectivism there will be a false freedom of speech, press and religion because anything that breaks the unity of the universal brotherhood of man such as traditional moral values or the Gospel will be banned as some sort of politically incorrect hate speech. And in this utopian collectivism no one has to work a day in their lives because everyone on Earth deserves an equal share of the world's wealth and resources whether they work or not because of the new moral rule of the universal brotherhood of man, and if anyone does want to volunteer to do some job, one will not be paid, or if one is paid, one's paycheck will be handed out equally to all the people of the world.

This "third way" system of world government is called the new Radicalism or Social Justice Liberalism, which means Socialist "Justice" utopianism where everyone is to live in selfless volunteer service for the collective, again, based on the single false "moral" standard of the universal brotherhood of man. This socialism is usually accompanied by a one-world false religion that has only two core beliefs, namely, the universal fatherhood of God and the same universal brotherhood of man, and these Two Great Falsehoods replace the Two Great Commandments of love God with all your heart mind and soul, and love your neighbor as yourself, which are sometimes thrown out as evil and if not, the Two Great Commandments are just placed over to the side and forgotten about because they are to be superseded by the new Two Great Falsehoods just as positive economic rights supersede and negate traditional individual rights.

In this new Liberal Christianity, whose purpose is the evil of Social Justice, Christ did *not* die on the Cross for our sins but to reconcile us to each other to end so-called "tribalism" or to, in effect, establish the good ole universal brotherhood of man and to "reconcile" man to himself! You cannot make this stuff up, but this is often, tragically, the official **religious** position of the Liberal apostate church, the Laodicean church, and Mystery Babylon or the Whore of Babylon of Revelation. The Liberal, utopian socialist-democrat **political** position is the Democrat Party in the US and the Labour Party in the UK, both of which have Social Justice and its phony positive rights as their sole reason for being based on the totally phony morality of the family of man or the universal brotherhood of man. Oh, the demonic tragedy of it all!

Fourth Formulation:
Global Corporatism
There is a fourth New World Order counter-millennialism to Judeo-Christian millennialism, and it is the millennialism of the EU and of G. H. W. Bush (senior), which for Bush is *also* based on humanism, the family of man or, in essence, the universal brotherhood of man.

This New World Order globalism is not socialist but more to fascist. It is sometimes called Global Corporatism. It is again based not on God and rights from God but on humanism and the family of man. Some of these type of globalists are said to add

Lucifer worship to the family of man, but there is no clear evidence that Bush was overtly associated with that. This globalism seeks to end free sovereign states and borders, but it does not seek to do worldwide collectivist Social Justice, but rather it tends to be a rule by private multinational corporations and unelected commissions controlling all economic and legal affairs and controlling all education and all media.

In this Global Corporatism "populism" becomes an evil as do, yet again, traditional concepts of freedom of speech, press, and religion. In the New World Order of Global Corporatism everything must be politically correct and tolerant, and there must be unity in promotion of moral hedonism in personal living and in promotion of a highly destructive radical multiculturalism in the society more generally. And there will be no borders and effectively no sovereign nation-states because this is all done, yet again, with an open disdain for free sovereign states with traditional concepts of Justice and Righteousness based on the moral Laws of Nature and of Nature's God, Wisely applied by the statesman legislator for the common good or general welfare.

Bottom line: "Globalism" is, indeed, generally a totally open movement of goods, services, capital, and people around the globe, but this inevitably undermines free sovereign states, and by its very nature globalism requires a one-world governmental authority to regulate things. In truth, almost invariably the globalist holds either to some form of a "New World Order" of Wells, FDR, and the United Nations to do worldwide Social Justice or to some form of a "New World Order" of globalist corporatism of transnational corporations. And often one sees a combination of these two forms of humanistic globalism.

In both of these two types of globalism borders and the free sovereign state are seen as evils and so are traditional concepts of private property and free enterprise and traditional concepts of Justice and Righteousness based on the moral Laws of Nature and of Nature's God of the 1688 and 1776 revolutions, and this is just as the "third way" social-democrat Liberals held to start this whole mess about 150 years ago well prior to World War I.

So, today in most if not all schools and churches we hear endlessly about the supposed good of hedonism, love as lawlessness, open borders, destructive radical multiculturalism, and the entire Social Justice agenda of a utopian New World Order based on the social-democrat positive rights of Wells, FDR and the UN to make us all equal. This tends to include outrageous politically correct nonsense on virtually every matter under the sun from gender identity to global warming hysteria, all of which are promoted in the schools, churches, and media just as Wells and FDR had planned in the early 1940s before they set up the UN to these ends.

Worldwide Pushback:
National Sovereignty Movements

Today we see a pushback against all forms of *false* New World Order globalism for the *true* New World Order vision of the American founders. This true Judeo-Christian millennial vision has free sovereign states worldwide in harmonious interaction in a millennialism world order of Locke and Jefferson and of the revolutions of 1688 and 1776 and of the Fifth Monarchists more generally.

And, indeed, it would appear this pushback by the saints in Christ is *also* a fulfillment of Bible prophecy and of Revelation 19 in particular just as much as Liberal and humanist politicians of globalism and lawlessness are a fulfillment of Bible prophecy concerning one-world government and one-world religion, where Christianity is in the Great Apostasy with another Jesus and another Gospel. This end-time, demonically deceived Christianity is clearly the lukewarm, tolerant Laodicean Church playing the Whore of Babylon with Babylon being tyrannical and totalitarian one-world humanistic government of the globalists, whether of the United Nations or otherwise.

(For more information on this see the booklets "UNDERSTANDING All Bible Prophecy" and "UNDERSTANDING Revelation 19")

===

Other booklets on the Reign of Christ in this UNDERSTANDING Series:

UNDERSTANDING Prophecy Fulfillment:
The Great Apostasy, Babylon, Mystery Babylon & the Reign of Christ

This little booklet gives an overview of the central major prophecies concerning the possible soon coming Reign of Christ. Specifically these are the prophecies of the Great Apostasy, Babylon, Mystery Babylon, and the man of lawlessness. These prophecies are seen as fulfilled in the false millennial visions of Marx and of the New World Order of UN Agenda 21 and Agenda 2030 and in the Liberal World Council of Churches.

UNDERSTANDING All Bible Prophecy:
Genesis to Revelation

This booklet holds that all prophecy should be interpreted in terms of the larger story of the Bible and the larger story of the Christian cosmology from the Creation to the Final Judgment, and this is especially the case for the book of Revelation.

UNDERSTANDING Globalism:
What is the "New World Order"?

This booklet looks at what "globalism" is generally and at the related topic of a "New World Order" that actually has *very* specific definitions and formulations that are often not well-known.

UNDERSTANDING Revelation 19:
Victory over One-World Government and One-World Religion

Revelation 19 though very controversial is actually very straightforward. The saints in a Marriage Supper of the Lamb move into a new more mature, intimate, and complete relationship with Christ, and then the saints in Christ and Christ in the saints completely and totally defeat the evils of one-world government and one-world religion. Simple enough when you get right down to it.

UNDERSTANDING Statesmanship
Classical Justice *versus* Social Justice

Probably no two notions are more misunderstood as well as more necessary to understand in our time than classical Justice and Social Justice. This booklet looks at the history of these two terms and how one stands for the Justice of statesmanship for doing the common good and the other for the injustice of special interest groups and wealth redistribution as a false human right for economic equality.

UNDERSTANDING Alternative
Political Universes:
The Natural Revelation & Self-Evident Truths

For some folks as Jefferson and the American founders, the Natural Law or so-called Higher Moral Law is a self-evident truth, but for others with a reprobate mind and no common sense, this is not the case at all. These modern-day people who have lost their common sense are just as the ancient Epicureans (atheist hedonists) while modern-day Liberals are just as ancient Gnostics with their false enlightenment and false morality. Understand these things, and you will pretty well understand Alternative Political Universes.

UNDERSTANDING Illegal Immigration:
The Wall and All It Stands For

"The Wall" of Donald Trump stands for many larger issues from exposing hypocrisy among professional politicians to ending globalism, open borders, and the often total lawlessness of our time. Lawlessness of the Liberal and atheist-humanist is, in fact, the spirit of anti-Christ.

UNDERSTANDING The Whole Counsel of the Kingdom:
The Central Message of Jesus and Paul

Both Jesus and Paul preached a Whole Counsel of the Kingdom message, but this is not a generally well-known truth. This booklet looks at the concept of a Whole Counsel of the Kingdom Christianity and what it entails, namely, true worship of God in Spirit and Truth as well as Just and Righteous government.

UNDERSTANDING Spiritual Warfare:
Satan as a Roaring Lion

Scripture tells us that Satan goes about like a roaring lion seeking whom he may devour, but this is generally not a very understood warning, and tragically many people, if not devoured completely, get an arm or leg eaten (so to speak). To be forewarned is to be forearmed. This booklet deals with ways to recognize and deal with demons.

===

All of the above booklets are part of a series on key issues of our time on the Reign of Christ at
www.ashiningcityonahill.org
www.reignofchrist.org

All of the above booklets are put together is a single **Volume I** called

UNDERSTANDING
The Reign of CHRIST:
The One Big Issue of Our Time
Volume I

This Volume I of all the above booklets together as well as all of the above booklets separately are available at **amazon.com**

www.ingramcontent.com/pod-product-compliance
Lightning Source LLC
Chambersburg PA
CBHW070106260726

48658CB00002B/1006